What Now Lord?

Lord, I have given my life to you.
What do I do now?

10 Steps to Christian Maturity

Dr. Michael Woods

PRESS

What Now Lord?
Lord, I have given my life to you. What do I do now?
10 Steps to Christian Maturity
by Dr. Michael Woods

Printed in the United States of America

ISBN 978-1-60791-178-4

www.xulonpress.com

Brenda:

Thank you for being a wonderful woman of God. May God bless you, Ocen, and your family with good health and abundant wealth.

M.D. Wood

Acknowledgements

I thank God for the unending supply of grace and mercy He has bestowed upon me. Thirty two years ago, He saved me from a life that was going nowhere in a hurry and made me His beloved son. I thank God for my wife Marilyn, for her prayers, her patience and her support over the years. If it were not for her, I would not be the man I am and neither would I have accomplished the things that I have achieved. I thank God for my children Danita, Dontevius and Danielle. I also thank God for my son in-law Donnell and my grandchildren, Deja, Destini and Da'Miya, for they have brought so much joy and happiness into my life.

Commendations

D r. Michael Woods writes out of an abundance of professional and practical experience. His work is a great contribution to the body of Christian literature and the body of Christ. I highly recommend its reading.
James Flanagan, Ph.D., President, Luther Rice Seminary – Atlanta, GA

Dr. Michael Woods' approach to Christian maturity is holistic as he combines faith with practice. His work of "studying theology" is reflected and mirrored by his life of "doing theology." This multifaceted examination of Christian discipleship will benefit any believer who is serious about going from "faith to faith" and "glory to glory." I highly recommend it.
Dr. Robert Smith, Jr. - Professor of Preaching Beeson Divinity School of Samford University - Birmingham, AL

A Preacher and a Professor with a Pastor's heart; Dr. Michael Woods' new book, "What Now Lord?" is written from a unique vantage point. Whether you are a new Christian or a mature saint of God, "What Now Lord?" will help you get to the next level in your walk of faith. I highly recommend Dr. Woods' new book to help you grow and achieve Ministry with Excellence.

J. Marcus Merritt - State Missionary
Alabama Baptist State Board of Missions - Office of Evangelism – Montgomery, AL

Dr. Michael Woods is one of those rare voices who consistently teaches and preaches relevant and practical truths. He never knew that I listened to him regularly on a local religious station. Our friendship has grown as we traveled together to the Holy Land. He has taught at my church and the Kingdom of God is richer because of his gift.

Dr. William E. Flippin – Greater Piney Grove Baptist Church – Atlanta, GA

"What now Lord?" is a question that I believe all new converts ask themselves. How do I begin this journey, and can I complete it successfully? Lord, what am I called to do? How do I discover my spiritual gifts, and fulfill my mission in life? "What Now Lord?" will answer many of these all important questions. It is an excellent tool for Christian discipleship. Not only will this book answer these questions, but will give the believer the tools to achieve the goal of spiritual maturity. Dr. Woods is a gifted man of God

who teaches with depth and clarity and you will be blessed by his work.
Pastor Edwin Newkirt – Church of God of Prophecy – Mt. Vernon, NY

Dr. Michael Woods and I graduated from the same theology school and have ministered together at various times. I have invited him into my pulpit to preach, and I believe in his ministry. I would recommend this work to new believers, new member courses, and discipleship studies.
Dr. Johnny Ellison - Green Acres Baptist Church - Warner Robins, GA

Michael Woods is one of the most thoughtful and biblical persons I know. Millions of people open the door of their lives to Jesus Christ; yet, some do not understand the fundamental difference in becoming a Christian and being a Christian."What Now Lord? provides a helpful and refreshing look at Christian growth. It will help shape your faith.
Pastor Dallas Scales - Word of Hope Fellowship – Greensboro, NC

Dr. Michael Woods is a great communicator of the gospel. I am proud to call him a friend and brother for over 17 years, and I congratulate him on his accomplishment of the writing of this book, "What Now Lord?" This book will bless, challenge, enlighten, and motivate new and struggling converts to a brand new way of thinking, believing and identification as Christians. I find the topics timely, concise and clear as we are faced with many untruths and challenges about Christ Jesus, the Bible, Christianity, Baptism, Tithes and Offerings, the Church and our Faith in God. I warmly recommend the reading of this book. **Dr. J. Carl Rahming - St Paul Baptist Church – Nassau, Bahamas**

Table of Contents

Introduction

Do you really understand what it means to be a Christian? Are you aware of who you are in the Lord and how the Lord looks upon you? Have you begun to understand how special you are to the Lord? Would you like to have a vibrant and intimate prayer life? Do you want to experience the blessings of God through your study of His Word?

Many persons have received Christ as their Savior, but have yet to experience the promises of Scripture, and neither do they live in the power of the Holy Spirit. In this power-packed and easy to read book, Dr. Woods addresses these issues and others that enable the believer to enter into the fullness of the Christian life. As you read and take heed to the teachings of this writing, you will learn how to walk in harmony with God, how to enjoy the promises made to the believer and how to engage the power of the Holy Spirit while facing the issues of life. May you be abundantly blessed by *What Now Lord?* and may you share your joy with others.

Chapter 1

Why Does the World Need a Savior?

Genesis 1:26-27

> *Then God said, "Let Us make man in Our image, according to Our likeness: let them have dominion over the fish of the sea, over the birds of the air, and over the cattle, over all the earth, and over every creeping thing that creeps on the earth." So God created man in his own image, in the image of God He created him; male and female He created them.*

Adam and Eve were created by God in His image and after His likeness. In addition, they were given the ability to reproduce children who would be born with their same nature, character and human capacities (Genesis 1:26-2:25). Originally, Adam and Eve were sinless and free to engage in a face-to-face relationship with God. They were placed in the

Garden of Eden and given numerous trees as sources for their vegetarian diet. There was the tree of life that would extend their existence forever and there was also the tree of the knowledge of good and evil that would produce death. Along with those privileges, God also gave our first parents the freedom of choice. They could choose to honor and obey God or they could choose to rebel against God. As much as God loved Adam and Eve, He wanted them to love Him in return with a conscious and willing heart. You see, true love only exists where a person has the choice to exercise that love or to do otherwise. True obedience and submission only exists where there is the choice to disobey and rebel. God wanted Adam and Eve to be faithful and loving toward Him. In spite of that, God gave Adam and Eve the privilege to choose their own course of life. The Scripture shows that, though they were enticed, Adam and Eve made the choice to reject God's way and to follow the agenda of Satan (Genesis 3:1-8; Revelation 12:9).

To some Bible readers, Adam and Eve's eating of the forbidden fruit seemed like a matter as simple as one eating an apple, but it was a far more profound matter than that. The Serpent challenged God's integrity, and thereby, brought suspicion upon God's very nature of holiness and sinless perfection. Adam and Eve accepted the Serpent's suggestions and followed Satan's leading. They ate from the Tree of the Knowledge of Good and Evil and experienced some very serious and far reaching results (Genesis 3:7-24). Consider this listing:

1. Adam and Eve lost their sense of innocence and unashamedness as described in Genesis 2:25. The beauty they saw in each other degenerated to embarrassment; so much so that they attempted to cover themselves with leaves. What had been described by God as good (Genesis 1:31) became something far less (Genesis 3:7).

2. Adam and Eve's desire to fellowship with God so declined that they attempted to hide themselves from God (Genesis 3:8; John 3:19-21).

3. Upon being questioned about their disobedience, both persons attempted to justify themselves. Adam blamed Eve for his disobedience and Eve blamed the Serpent for her non-compliance (Genesis 3:9-13).

4. Originally, it seemed as if childbirth was to be a pleasant and pain-free experience. Also, Eve's rank with Adam was more of a functional equal. After they sinned against God, He rebuked Eve by decreeing that she would experience great pain during childbirth. In addition, God relegated her relational status to being under the authority of her husband. The edict of painful childbirths carried over to the delivery of all children. Adam's authority over his wife was also applied to all marital relationships (Genesis 3:16; Ephesians 5:22-24).

5. The earth was cursed and it lost its global Eden-like environment. It became a rugged environment that required much work to live in and great toil to produce food and life-supporting resources (Genesis 3:17-18).

6. Adam was cursed to an existence of hard labor in order to produce the necessities of life and, in the end, he would eventually die. This implied that, in order to facilitate death, Adam and Eve would experience physical decline and sickness (Genesis 3:19; Hebrews 9:27).

7. Adam and Eve were permanently banished from the Garden of Eden. This action would surely lead to death because they would no longer have access to the Tree of Life that provided immortality. Also, their expulsion implied the ending of their intimate and face-to-face fellowship with God. This banishment and loss of face-to-face interaction with God may have signaled the beginning of the practice we call "prayer" (Genesis 3:22-24).

The Need for the Savior

Adam and Eve's sins not only caused them to loose the beautiful environment of Eden, but they corrupted their entire being; body, soul and spirit. Their corruption would cause their children and all future offspring to be born corrupt and alienated from God (Psalm 51:5; Ephesians 2:1-3). The earth was cursed and it degenerated from its initial quality to a place of toil and sorrow. The harmony that existed between man and animal was replaced by a sense of fear between both. More importantly, the relationship that existed between God and man became seriously compromised. Adam and Eve lost what may have been the privilege of having face-to-face contact with God.

From the time of this debacle in the Garden of Eden, the Bible began promising a Savior who would redeem man and the earth from all of the curses placed upon them. In Genesis 3:15, the Savior was referred to as the "Seed of the Woman." This title was used because Jesus would be born of a woman but without the involvement of a man. In Isaiah 7:14, that idea was expanded upon as Jesus was described as one who would be born of a virgin. In John 1:14, Jesus was said to have been specifically generated or begotten of God the Father. In Matthew 1:20, the conception of Jesus was said to have been caused by the Holy Sprit. In summary, Jesus was God almighty who manifested in the flesh to die for the sins of the world and was resurrected to confirm His deity and eternal nature (1 Timothy 3:16).

Conclusion

God desired the best for Adam and Eve and He desires the best for us. Jesus was the best gift God could give to humankind (John 3:16). Jesus offers us the best gifts available; the gift of eternal life (Romans 6:23), and the gift of faith through which we access God's eternal life (Ephesians 2:8-9). The sins of Adam and Eve demanded a Savior and Jesus is that Savior who offers redemption to all mankind.

An unsaved man talked with a minister about how to become a Christian because he was deeply

convicted about his life and lifestyle. When he asked the minister what he had to do in order to become saved, the minister told him that he was too late. The man responded, "Too late! What do you mean? Do you mean that I am too late to be saved?" The minister then said, "No, you're just too late to do anything yourself. Christ died for your sins and has already done everything that can be done."

—*Author Unknown*

Chapter 2

What is a Christian?

Acts 11:26
And the disciples were first called Christians
in Antioch.

The word "Christian" points to a person who is a follower of Jesus Christ. Both secular and religious histories recognize Jesus as the greatest and most revered person who has ever lived upon this earth. More research has been done on Jesus and more publications and presentations have been produced about Him than any other person. In the Bible, Jesus is presented not just as a great teacher but as the Son of God and as the Creator Himself. In some kind of mysterious way, He entered the human sphere and lived as a man (John 1:1-14; 1 Timothy 3:16). Not only did He live in a body as a man but, He also experienced a mortal death as other men do.

Death ends the history of humans but death was not the end of the life and times of Jesus Christ because

He was resurrected from the dead. Eyewitnesses, both friend and foe, testified that Jesus rose from the dead and that He confirmed His resurrection with many infallible proofs (Luke 24:1-35; Acts 1:1-2). Though the Romans and the Jews of His time had investigative bureaus that were second to none, no evidence whatsoever could be produced to refute the claims of the resurrection of the Son of God. All of the facts and evidences point to Jesus Christ being all that the Bible describes Him to be and even more. In view of those truths, the greatest earthly association one can have is to be connected to Jesus Christ and the greatest title a human being can acquire is to be called a Christian.

Are Any Persons Born Christians?

Many persons call themselves Christians or are classified by others as Christians simply because they were born to parents who were Christians. The truth of the matter is that the faith and religious standing of parents do not transfer to the child. As explained in the previous chapter, all persons are born spiritually alienated from God (Psalm 51:1-5) and none are automatically born Christian. All humans come into this world as selfish persons who have little or no desire to submit to authority, even God's authority. Children do not have to be taught to become angry, to be self-centered, to say bad words, or to engage in sinful behavior. We all were born with a leaning toward unrighteousness. Out parents had the responsibility and challenge of teaching us about God and to instruct us to be honest and to do what was good and right. They soon discovered that it was not easy to ingrain godly principles into the hearts and minds of their offspring.

One evening Jesus encountered a man by the name of Nicodemus. This man had been born into a religious family and had ascended to high rank in the religious community of the Jews. Nicodemus was a teacher, he was wealthy and was benevolent with his resources. Though he had all of those things going for him, he was destitute of a real, life-changing relationship with God. Though Jesus was very cordial toward him, He told Nicodemus that he needed to be born again or he would not enter into God's kingdom. Nicodemus had been born one time of his parents but, Jesus told him that he had to experience another birth into a new life; one that could only be facilitated by the Holy Spirit (John 3:1-16). When a person becomes born again, he begins following the teachings and examples of Jesus Christ, thereby, earning the distinction of being called a "Christian."

How Does One Become a Christian?

Someone said that becoming a Christian was as easy as ABC. Though that sounds very simple, there is a little more to the matter than that acronym. What are the elements that lead to a person becoming a Christian?

Acknowledgement

The Bible states that all humans are born with a condition defined as "sin." This means that humans have a natural leaning toward thoughts, words and deeds that are contrary to God's will. It also means that we are naturally selfish and uninterested in surrendering ourselves to any authority, including the authority of God. That is the emphasis of King David's statement in Psalm 51:5: *"Behold, I was brought forth in iniquity, And in sin my mother conceived me."* David was not saying that his mother was engaging in an act of sin when she became pregnant with him. David was saying that he was born spiritually alienated from God and absent of a right relationship with his Creator. It is this sinful and alienated condition that a person must acknowledge in order to begin the transition that results in one becoming a Christian.

Repentance

A person who desires to become a Christian must be willing to turn to God and to ready himself to follow the Word of God. Repentance also has the idea of a person turning from all behavior he knows to be wrong and sinful. The root word "repent" or other forms of it were very prominent in the teaching and preaching of Jesus and the Apostles; so much so that it is found at least 64 times in the New Testament. This word has to do with a person "changing his mind about a matter and evidencing his changed mind by a change in his behavior."

Imagine a person driving on the freeway intending to reach an important destination but discovering that he had been traveling in the wrong direction. That person will acknowledge his error and confirm that acknowledgement by taking the next exit and then re-entering the freeway going in the opposite direction. So it is with repentance. In order to become a Christian, a person must recognize that he has been traveling down the road of life in the wrong direction. He must confirm that recognition by turning to God. By doing so, he turns his mind and heart from those things he had been doing that were against the will of God (Mark 1:14-15; Acts 3:19).

Belief

All persons have beliefs and all persons have faith in one thing or another. Becoming a Christian has to do with a person placing his faith in Jesus Christ and in all that the Bible says about Him. Jesus was born of a virgin, lived a sinless life, died a substitutionary death, was buried and arose from the dead. Those are the primary elements of the gospel. When faith is placed in Jesus Christ and in those details of the gospel, the new birth process is furthered (Romans 10:9-10; Acts 16:30-31).

Confession

Not only must a person place his faith and belief in Jesus Christ, he must also acknowledge to God that Jesus is the Savior and the only way an individual can become born again (John 14:6; Acts 4:10-12). Words of confession must be stated to God, by the person desiring to become a Christian. This is what is known as the "Sinner's Prayer." It is the verbalization of an individual's acknowledgement of the truth of the gospel, his repentance and, the placing of his faith in Jesus Christ. It also includes his confession that Jesus is his only way to God, and his asking God to save him and come and live in his heart. Following is an example:

Lord, I admit that I am a lost sinner and that I need you in my life. I am sorry for all the things I have done wrong over my entire life and I am ready to turn from those things. I believe that Jesus died for my sins so that I could be saved. I confess that He is Lord and Savior and I can only be saved through Him. Please come into my life, please save me and please make me your child.

Conclusion

Though four elements have been mentioned that facilitate the new birth (acknowledgement, repentance, belief and confession), all are done simultaneously and in the same setting. When they are done with sincerity and honesty, a miracle occurs. A person is brought into right relationship with God the Father, he becomes a member of the Church (the Body of Christ), and he becomes indwelt by the Holy Spirit. This person then has more than religion. He now has a life-changing relationship with his Creator that will transform his life for the rest of his life (2 Corinthians 5:17; 1 John 4:12-13; 1 Peter 2:1-2).

A Christian is:

    A mind through which Christ thinks.
    A voice through which Christ speaks.
    A heart through which Christ loves.
    A hand through which Christ helps.
                  —Author Unknown

Chapter 3

How Do I Grow into a Mature Christian?

1 Peter 2:1-2

Therefore, laying aside all malice, all deceit, hypocrisy, envy, and all evil speaking, as newborn babes, desire the pure milk of the word, that you may grow thereby.

One summer day back in 1993, I spent about tree hours in my yard, cutting the grass and trimming shrubbery. When I was done, I had two matters on my mind. I was both tired and hungry. First I decided to rest in the den for a while and then to make myself a snack afterwards. As I was sitting in my most comfortable chair, my youngest daughter who was seven at the time, came to me and asked, "What's wrong daddy?" I told her that I was tired and I was hungry. She then told me to rest while she made me a sandwich. I told her not to worry about it and that I would make the sandwich myself after

I had rested a while. My daughter gently pressed me back into the chair and insisted that she make the sandwich. I had three primary thoughts in my mind. First, I had not ever seen her make a sandwich before. Second, I did not want to eat a sandwich and act as if it was good when it was not. Third, I had just spent three hours manicuring the lawn and I did not want to have to spend additional time cleaning the kitchen. In spite of those thoughts, I relented and welcomed my daughter to prepare the sandwich. A few minutes later, my daughter brought me a beautiful turkey sandwich with lettuce and tomatoes on a paper plate and a soda in a paper cup. As I ate the sandwich it was as delicious as any I had ever eaten. When I was done, I went into the kitchen and deposited the plate and cup into the trash and observed that the kitchen was spotless. I immediately went to my daughter, thanked her for the sandwich, gave her a hug and a kiss and told her that I loved her. It was at that time that I realized that my daughter, who had entered this life as a liability, was growing up and becoming an asset. This little girl who had required so much energy and attention from everyone else in the house was maturing and becoming able to make meaningful contributions toward the well-being of the home and family.

So it is for every person who accepts Jesus as Savior and enters the Christian family. No matter what age we were when we became born again, we all became babes in Christ. We lacked the knowledge of Scripture to defend the faith against those who promote evolution, Buddhism and other false belief systems. We lacked the maturity to engage in intense spiritual warfare and to live victoriously over the enemies of our spiritual wellbeing. Therefore, it is incumbent upon every believer to pursue a course of life and a course of learning that will help each of us become strong men and women in the faith who can help others come to know the Lord and become strong believers in the Lord also. In the interest of making meaningful progress in this area of concern, consider the teachings of 1 Peter 2:1-2 to see what instructions this passage offers that will help us grow into mature men and women of God.

1. *We Must <u>Abstain</u> from Activities that are Contrary to the Word of God!*

In the first clause of 1 Peter 2:1, Peter said, "Therefore, laying aside all malice, all deceit, hypocrisy, envy, and all evil speaking..." In this statement, Peter used the words *malice, deceit, hypocrisy, envy* and *evil speaking* to represent the three ways we sin; with our thoughts, our words and our deeds. In this phrase the word *all* is used three times. The primary idea being communicated is that if you and I expect to grow and mature in the Lord, we must abstain from every activity that is contrary to the Word of God. In Hebrews 12:1-2, the same idea is stated in this way:

Hebrews 12:1-2
Therefore we also, since we are surrounded by so great a cloud of witnesses, let us lay aside every weight, and the sin which so easily ensnares us, and let us run with endurance the race that is set before

us, looking unto Jesus the author and finisher of our faith, who for the joy that was set before Him endured the cross, despising the shame, and has sat down at the right hand of the throne of God.

Let me further illustrate this truth in this way. Several years ago, I identified a spot of land on which I wanted to plant a garden. As I looked at that land, I visualized myself harvesting corn, cucumbers, tomatoes, cantaloupes and a host of other fruits and vegetables, but I had a major problem. The garden spot I was observing was covered with bushes, weeds and kudzu vines. So I called a man to clear the land and prepare the ground for planting. He first used his tractor to cut down all of the weeds and bushes. He then plowed the dirt and laid out rows where I could set out plants and plant seeds. When he was done, he said, "Now your garden is ready for you to sow seed." I knew it would be a waste of time and energy to place tomato plants and plant vegetable seeds in the midst of the bushes and weeds because they would choke out the crops, and keep them from growing to maturity and bearing fruit. Therefore, the first thing I did was lay aside all of the things in the garden area that would hinder growth and maturity of fruit-bearing plants.

In like manner, if you want to grow into a mature Christian, you must lay aside all activities that are contrary to the teachings of the Bible. There may be someone you associate with who is a negative influence. There may be places you go where negative activities are routine. If you want to be a growing believer who can strengthen other believers and influence non-Christians to follow Jesus Christ, you must abstain from all activities that are contrary to the Word of God.

2. *We Must Harbor a Baby-Like <u>Attitude</u> Toward the Word of God!*

In the first clause of 1 Peter 2:2, we find this phrase, "…as newborn babes…" The idea here is that in order for you to be a growing and maturing believer you must harbor the same attitude of humility that is found in newborn babies. Babies are not arrogant nor do they act as if they are independent and have no need for others. Newly-born infants realize how helpless they are and they know how badly they need the attention of others for their basic needs. Therefore, they cry out; especially when their stomachs are empty and their diapers are full. You must maintain this same mental disposition of humbleness toward God and toward your pastor. God will use the preaching and teaching ministries of the church you attend to inform you and educate you in the promises and in the requirements of Scripture. You must be eager to learn, and be faithful in your attendance in order to gain the biblical knowledge and the maturity produced by Scripture. In 1 Peter 5:5-6, the Apostle Peter teaches this same truth in this way:

<u>1 Peter 5:5-6</u>
Likewise you younger people, submit yourselves to your elders. Yes, all of you be submissive to one another, and be clothed with humility, for "God

*resists the proud, But gives grace to the humble."
Therefore humble yourselves under the mighty hand
of God, that He may exalt you in due time.*

God will lift you up and raise you to another level
of competence and confidence in your Christian
walk as you realize that you cannot have a fruitful
and productive life apart from being dedicated to the
Lord (John 15:1-8). As you humble yourself under the
authority of God and His Word, you will be equipped
and empowered to live a victorious Christian life.

*3. We Must Maintain a Healthy <u>Appetite</u> for the
Word of God!*

In this second clause in 1 Peter 2:2, we find the
phrase, "...desire the pure milk of the word...".
The emphasis being made here is that in order for
Christians to progress from spiritual infancy toward
maturity, they must possess a healthy appetite for
the Word of God. This means that you must make
personal Bible study a priority. A good practice to
engage in is to spend time in prayer at the beginning
of your day. After praying, spend some time reading
Scripture. There are resources that separate the Bible
into 365 sections that enable you to read through the
entire Scripture in one year. You can use the passage
your pastor preached from the previous Sunday. The
Sunday School or the Bible Study lesson can be used
as a morning meditation text. If you did not complete
the New Member Class at your church, you need to
make doing so a priority. If your church has Sunday
School, Bible Study, Discipleship Groups, Cell

Groups or other settings where you can be taught the Scripture, your regular attendance in some of those settings will greatly enhance your Christian experience. In addition, be selective about the sources you look to for entertainment. The teachings of the Scripture are going to encourage you to pursue a life of Christ-likeness. If the music you listen to, the television programs you watch and the movies you go to suggest activities and behaviors that are contrary to Scripture, they are going to hinder your growth and keep you in bondage to the very lifestyle Jesus came to save you from. Consider the words of Jesus in the Gospel of Matthew:

Matthew 5:6
Blessed are those who hunger and thirst for righteousness, For they shall be filled.

When you were saved by the Lord you were also justified. This term means that you were declared righteous and placed in right relationship with your heavenly Father. From this position of righteousness, you are instructed to pursue the right kind of thinking and mental disposition (Philippians 2:5; Romans 12:1-2). You are instructed to pursue the right kind of speaking and language (Colossians 3:8). You are instructed to pursue the right kind of behavior (Ephesians 4:17-32). As we harbor a healthy appetite for the Word of God and pursue the teachings of the Word of God, we will experience God's power that enables us to grow into strong Christians who can provide an example worthy of others following.

Conclusion

Flowers are planted, watered and fertilized so they will grow and bloom with beauty. Fruits and vegetables are planted, watered and fertilized so they will grow and produce food. We were saved by the blood of Jesus, planted in the family of God, and watered and fertilized by the Word of God so we produce results that glorify God and bless those around us. What must we do to experience these desired results?

1. <u>Abstain</u> from all activities that are contrary to the Word of God!
2. Harbor a baby-like <u>Attitude</u> toward the Word of God!
3. Maintain a Healthy <u>Appetite</u> for the Word of God!

The last phrase in 1 Peter 2:2 says "…that you may grow thereby…" The idea being communicated is that as we do these three things, we will grow from spiritual infancy to spiritual maturity and become strong men and women in the Christian family. What are some of the indicators that we are growing toward maturity?

1. We will possess greater peace and joy as we deal with the issues of life.
2. We will be kinder and more loving to those around us.

3. We will possess a greater desire to spend time in prayer to God.
4. We will become more diligent in our private and public Bible study.
5. We will look forward to coming together with others to worship God.
6. We will harbor a growing love for God and His will.
7. We will be more inclined to tell others about our relationship with the Lord.
8. We will harbor a greater commitment to be honest and do what is right in God's sight.

Maturity is:

The ability to stick with a job until it is finished.
The ability to do a job without being supervised.
The ability to carry money without spending it.
The ability to bear an injustice without wanting to get even.

—Abigail Van Buren

Chapter 4

What About Water Baptism?

Acts 8:36-38
> *Now as they went down the road, they came to some water. And the eunuch said, "See, here is water. What hinders me from being baptized?" Then Philip said, "If you believe with all your heart, you may." And he answered and said, "I believe that Jesus Christ is the Son of God." So he commanded the chariot to stand still. And both Philip and the eunuch went down into the water, and he baptized him.*

Churches today provide water baptism for their members at varying intervals. Some baptize immediately upon a person receiving Christ. They have a pool that is always ready. They have robes, new undergarments and every other personal item to accommodate persons who did not come prepared for baptism immediately after receiving the Lord as Savior. On the other hand, there are churches that offer Baptism services once per year, once per quarter, once per month and at other intervals.

The Scripture indicates that water baptism was the first command directed to a person after that person became a Christian. The Scripture also indicates that water baptism was administered to the new convert as soon thereafter as was practical (Acts 2:41; 8:12; 8:36-38; 9:18; 10:48; 16:33). The apostles understood water baptism to have a very important connection to the transition of a person into the family of God; therefore, they saw no need to delay it. The baptism did not save anyone; but rather it communicated to the public that the person being baptized had become a Christian and had committed his life to following Jesus Christ.

In some modern settings, converts to Christ are required to complete certain classes or meet other qualifications before being baptized. In some churches, the greater the requirements, the longer the delay before the ordinance of Baptism is administered. As much as we should respect the wisdom of our church leaders, they should subordinate their wisdom to the words and practices of the apostles, as demonstrated in the book of Acts. The only thing Peter, Philip and the apostles required of a baptism candidate was genuine repentance from sins, belief in the gospel and faith in the Savior. Could we be in error by requiring anything more?

Water Baptism: What Does It Mean?

The word <u>baptize</u> literally means to "make whelmed." The connotation of this word in the Christian community has to do with "the placing of a person into water in such a way that he becomes overwhelmed or fully covered by the water." The baptism of Jesus by John the Baptist shows, Christ becoming completely immersed in the water (Matthew 3:13-17). God the Father immediately spoke of His pleasure with His Son's baptism. This infers that God was pleased with every aspect including the mode of baptism of Jesus being momentarily "buried or overwhelmed under the water." It seems that all of the baptisms recorded thereafter were by this same method of immersion (Acts 8:36-38).

In some churches, the minister uses the hand to sprinkle the candidate with water, some use a vessel to pour the water onto the candidate's head while others do not baptize at all. We must realize that some of the narratives in the Bible were left on record to serve as examples for us to follow. Finally, if the Christian life can be summed up in a repentant sinner seeking to think, speak and live as Jesus did, then we should emulate His actions in every way possible (Philippians 2:5; 1 John 2:6). If those things are true, the mode of water baptism is one of the first opportunities for the new convert to begin emulating his Lord and Savior.

What are the Spiritual Implications of Water Baptism?

Though in Scripture, the predominate use of the word "baptism" has to do with one being immersed into water, Jesus used the word in relation to His death (Mat. 20:20-23). From there, Paul made a mysterious association between the death, burial and resurrection of Jesus and the baptism of the believer (Romans 6:3-5). Though this passage also emphasizes the baptism of the Holy Spirit, that matter will be addressed later in this writing. The Romans passage indicates that Jesus was immersed into the state of death. His physical body did in fact expire and it experienced decease just as multitudes before Him. After His death, the body of the Lord was given a proper burial according to the customs of that day (Luke 23:50-53). After spending three days in the grave, He was resurrected to life and immortality. All of the gospel writers report those events and hundreds of persons were eye witnesses of this great miracle (Matthew 27:45-28:20; 1 Corinthians 15:1-8).

Romans 6:3-5 parallels the water baptism of the believer with the death, burial and resurrection of Christ. In many churches that practice baptism by immersion, the shape and form of the baptism pool is very similar to that of a grave. When water baptism is done by immersion, the candidate is momentarily buried under the water; representing his death to his old life of sin. When he is brought up, it is representative of a resurrection to a new life in the Lord. As the candidate walks away from the pool, doing so is representative of him walking in a new lifestyle; a life in accord with the teachings of Scripture. Water baptism can also be described as a public ceremony that celebrates an individual's new birth into the family of God (Acts 2:38-41).

What About the Baptism of the Holy Spirit?

The word "baptism" has the same connotation when referring to the ministry of the Holy Spirit as it does when it is associated with water. In each instance, the convert is being overwhelmed and immersed. 1 Corinthians 12:13 is one of the most definitive passages on the baptism of the Holy Spirit. In this passage, the apostle Paul said that every person who received Jesus as Savior was immersed or placed into the Body of Christ; God's Church. This baptism is performed by the Holy Spirit and the Holy Spirit alone. Just as water baptism is to be done once for life, the baptism of the Holy Spirit is done once for all time in the life of the believer. The baptism of the Holy Spirit is also permanent because it permanently placed the believer into the Christian family. This truth helps us to understand that water baptism is actually a celebration of one who has already been placed into the Body of Christ.

Who Should Be Baptized?

As has been stated previously, water baptism is the declaration of the believer that he has received Christ as Savior. It is also an act of obedience by one who recognizes Jesus as his Lord. It stands to reason that if an unbeliever is baptized, the event is meaningless to the Lord and to the person being baptized. If the person being baptized has not received Jesus as Savior, the event makes no redemptive statement to the world nor is it an act of obedience by one who has been placed into the body of Christ by the Holy Spirit. Persons who were baptized before they became Christians went through a ritual that did not really count for anything in the sight of God. Christians in this category need to consider these truths about water baptism. It would be to their advantage to submit themselves to a baptism ceremony that will make an accurate statement of their relationship with the Lord and one through which their obedience can be blessed by God.

Acts 8:26-40 may be one of the clearest illustrations in Scripture of the kind of water baptism ceremony that honors God and that brings blessings upon the candidate. In this narrative we find the following truths:

1. The Ethiopian was genuinely interested in matters relating to God. He demonstrated his interest by traveling to Jerusalem to worship God and by his reading of Scripture. He was not a baby being baptized with no awareness of the experience. He was not a young child being compelled by his parent or guardian. He was fully able to make his own decision about spiritual matters. See verses 26-28.
2. As Phillip explained the plan of salvation to the Ethiopian, he requested to be baptized, but he was told that he first had to become a believer in Jesus Christ. See verses 29-37.
3. The Ethiopian expressed his acceptance of Phillip's explanation of the gospel and he affirmed his belief in Christ as the Savior. See verse 37.

4. The Ethiopian then had the chariot to stop and Phillip immersed him in the water as an expression of his acceptance of Jesus as his Savior. See verse 38.

5. The Ethiopian went on his way expressing the joy of one who had been newly converted by the Lord Jesus Christ. See verse 39.

6. This entire encounter had been orchestrated by the Holy Spirit. Phillip had been led to this man by the Holy Spirit and had been miraculously transported to his next place of service by the Holy Spirit. From all indications, this Ethiopian had a genuine salvation experience and he engaged in a water baptism ceremony that pleased God.

Conclusion

This passage of Scripture may be able to serve as a litmus test for all water baptism ceremonies. The affirmations illustrated in this encounter between this African and this Hebrew should serve as a guide for all others who desire their baptism ceremony to be acceptable to God and to be an act of obedience than can contribute to the candidate's blessings from the Lord.

God uses broken things: broken soil and broken clouds to produce grain; broken grain to produce bread; broken bread to feed our bodies. He wants our stubbornness broken into humble obedience.
—The Vance Hanover Quote Book

Chapter 5

Can I Pray as Jesus Did?

Luke 11:1
> *Now it came to pass, as He was praying in a certain place, when He ceased, that one of his disciples said unto Him, "Lord, teach us to pray, as John also taught his disciples."*

It could be said that the greatest need of the Christian is to have on-going intimate fellowship with the Lord that is facilitated by his or her prayer life. During the time my son was a police officer, on some days I would watch him prepare for work. Sometimes he put on his gun belt and at other times he draped it over his shoulder. Occasionally he wore his bullet-proof vest and sometimes he carried it in his hand. There were times he even left some of his regalia at home, but he never left the house without putting on his radio. He always set it to the proper frequency and spoke to the dispatch to assure that he was connected to his home base. My son knew how vitally important it was for him to always have direct communications with headquarters. It is no different with those of us who have received the Lord as our Savior. We need an intimate prayer life that keeps us connected to God at all times so that we constantly receive directions and guidance from Him.

One day, after observing Jesus during His prayer time, His 12 disciples asked Him to teach them to pray as John the Baptist had taught his disciples. This request prompted the response we call the "Lord's Prayer" or the "Model Prayer" (Luke 11:1-4). This event occurred about a year and a half into the Lord's earthly ministry. His disciples had observed Him turn water into wine, heal sick persons, cast out demons, cleanse lepers, raise the dead, teach and preach with great profundity and do a host of other miraculous things. Though the apostles saw the Lord perform many miracles, they never asked Him to teach them to do any of those things, they simply asked Him to teach them how to intimately connect with God the Father as He did. Though the disciples were not men of great learning and scholarship, they were very intelligent persons. They were able to see that the power of Jesus' public ministry sprang out of His private prayer life. They understood that if they could connect with the Father as Jesus did, the Father would use them to perform miracles, just as He worked miraculously through Christ. Jesus confirmed their conclusions by telling them that they would do the same things He did and that they would do even greater works (John 14:12). Jesus would serve on earth for only three and a half years while some of them would serve three and a half decades. Therefore, their works would exceed Jesus' in quantity but none could exceed what the Lord did in quality. We need to learn this same lesson from the disciples as we pursue an intimate prayer life with the Lord. How do we engage in this process of the pursuit of the heart of God so that we are blessed by the mighty hand of God?

1. Realize that God loves us more than we even understand the meaning of love. He wants the very best for us and God is always looking for opportunities and occasions to bless us. As such, He has promised to supply every one of our needs and many of the desires of our hearts (Psalm 37:4; Philippians 4:19).

2. Approach God with absolute reverence for who He is. When praying, be as clear and as specific as you would when explaining to your physician your hurts and pains but realize that you are approaching the Architect of the universe. Therefore, honor God and show Him the respect He is due (Psalms 111:9; Luke 11:1-2).

3. Continually confess your sins to the Lord; both those you know of and those you have committed unknowingly (Proverbs 28:13; 1 John 1:8-9). Each of us need to realize that God's grace will always provide forgiveness for our sins, but His grace is not an excuse or a license to continue committing a particular sin (Romans 6:1-2). God's grace provides us with the opportunity to learn how to live the Christian life. As we do, each day we become less like Adam and more

like Christ. As a result, we are better able to live in victory over the Devil, over the influence of the world, and above our own human inclinations (Romans 8:29; Hebrews 12:1-2).

4. Once we pray to receive Jesus as Savior, we then have unlimited access to God's presence and to His throne of grace (Hebrews 4:14-16). In spite of that fact, each of us need to be mindful of the things that can impede our prayer requests and minimize the joy of our fellowship with God. What are some of those hindrances?

a. If we have sins and shortcomings that are not being surrendered to the Lord, our prayers can be hindered (Psalm 66:18; James 1:22-27). When we are sick and cannot rectify our situations with home remedies, usually we make an appointment to see the doctor. Upon meeting with the physician, we describe our symptoms, aches, pains and discomforts. We will confess all of our physical maladies, with faith that the doctor will write a prescription and give advisements that will heal us of our displeasurable conditions. Remember that God made us, He loves us and He wants us to be free of everything that can hinder our fellowship with Him. We need to tell Him all about your sins. He already knows everyone of them and He wants us to be honest and sincere with Him (Psalm 139:1-18). Confess your sins to the Lord and allow Him to cleanse you of all unrighteous thoughts, words and deeds. God will forgive us of our sins, He will give us victory over our shortcomings and He will cast our past deeds into the Sea of Forgetfulness (Psalm 103:8-13).

b. We must harbor a forgiving spirit toward others (Matthew 6:14-15). When we pray, we must do so realizing that anything can occur during the day that could hurt and offend us. Some of the persons we encounter often do not realize the extent of their unkindness and rudeness. On the other hand, there are a few persons in this sinful world who purposely perpetrate pain on others. The respect for Christianity is at an all time low, and some of us will be mistreated and disrespected simply because we serve the true and living God. Therefore, we must begin each day with a forgiving attitude. We must forgive the offenders we will encounter even before we encounter them (Psalm 5:1-3). As we extend forgiveness to others, God will freely extend forgiveness to us.

c. We must realize that we are not superior to others (Luke 18:9-14). Any of us can exalt ourselves by comparing ourselves to someone else. We can look at the degradation that is broadcast on the television news and see others as wicked and degenerate. We can get offended at church and view another Christian as being un-Christianlike. In spite of those realities, we must resist the temptation to think more highly of ourselves than we should (Romans 12:3). A superiority complex will cause us to become intoxicated with our own good behavior, thereby, blinding us to our faults and sins (Matthew 7:1-5). Jesus Christ is the standard of measurement for all Christians therefore, He is the One we should compare ourselves to and strive to be like (Ephesians 4:13). Certainly, we should be thankful that we are not the sinful persons we used to be, but we also need to admit that we have not yet become the persons we ought to be (Matthew 5:48). As we humble ourselves under God and His Word, He will facilitate our maturity and, in the final analysis, give us victory over all of our sins (1 Peter 5:5-7).

d. We must treat others right; beginning with those closest to us at home (1 Peter 3:7). Though this passage of Scripture specifically instructs husbands to properly treat their wives, the same behavior is expected of wives toward their husbands. Afterwards, we are to show the love of God toward everyone we encounter (Matthew 7:12). Jesus even said that the general public would be able to distinguish His disciples from others by the love we express through our character, our conversation and through our daily conduct (John 13:34-35).

e. We must pursue a life of obedience to the Lord. The Holy Spirit lives in the heart of every Christian and He seeks to manifest His holy character through us (Galatians 5:22-23). In order to enjoy this quality of life, we must make a daily effort to study the Scripture and obey God's Word in every area of life (2 Timothy 2:15; 3:15-16). As we discover things in our lives that are wrong, we are to ask God for forgiveness for our sins, refrain from ungodly activities and seek God's power so that we gain strength in our areas of weakness (Hebrews 12:1-2; 1 John 5:1-5).

Conclusion

Every believer can pray as Jesus did, connect with the Father as Jesus did, and receive strength and power from the Holy Spirit as Jesus did. Jesus' prayer in Matthew 6:9-13 and in Luke 11:1-4 was a model for us to follow so that we can pursue intimacy with God as He did and claim the benefits promised by God. Make payer a priority in your life. Pray when you get up each morning. Pray all throughout the day. Pray before you turn in each night. If you cannot sleep during the night, seize the opportunity to have a time of intimacy and fellowship with the Lord, for the Bible says in Luke 18:1, "…Men always ought to pray and not lose heart!"

Be Lord,
> **within me to strengthen me, without me to guard me, over me to shelter me, beneath me to establish me, before me to guide me, after me to forward me, round me to secure me.**

> **—Lancelot Andrews**

Chapter 6

Can I Read and Understand My Bible?

Psalm 119:105
Your word is a lamp unto my feet And a light
to my path.

The greatest expression of God's love to us was shown in the giving of His Son as our Savior and the giving of His Holy Spirit as our Sustainer. After the Son of God and the Spirit of God, the next greatest gift to us from heaven is the Holy Scripture. Consider this tribute to the Bible from Finis J. Dake:

The Bible is not an amulet, a charm, a fetish, or a book that will work wonders by its very presence. It is a book that will work wonders in every life, here and hereafter, if acted upon and obeyed in faith and in sincerity. It is God's inspired revelation of the origin and destiny of all things, written in the most simple human language possible so that the most unlearned can understand and obey its teachings. It is self-interpreting and covers every subject of human knowledge and need now and forever.

As a literary composition, the Bible is the most remarkable book ever made. It is a divine library of 66 books, some of considerable size, and others no larger than a tract. These books include various forms of literature – history, biography, poetry, proverbial sayings, hymns, letters, directions for elaborate ritualistic worship, laws, parables, riddles, allegories, prophecies, drama, and others. They embrace all manner of literary styles in human expression.

It is the book that reveals the mind of God, the state of man, the way of salvation, the doom of sinners, and the happiness of believers. Its doctrines are holy, its precepts binding, its histories true, and its decisions immutable. Read it to be wise, believe it to be safe, and practice it to be holy. The Bible contains light to direct you food to support you, and comfort to cheer you. It is the travelers map, the pilgrim's staff, the pilot's compass, the soldier's sword, and the Christian's charter. Here heaven is opened, and the gates of hell disclosed. Christ is its grand subject, our good is its design, and the glory of God its end. It should fill your memory, rule your heart, and guide your feet in righteousness and true holiness. Read it slowly, frequently, prayerfully, meditatively, searchingly, devotionally, and study it constantly, perseveringly, and industriously. Read it through and through until it becomes a part of your being and generates faith that will move mountains.

The Bible is a mine of wealth, the source of health, and a world of pleasure. It is given to you in this life, will be opened at the judgment, and will stand forever. It involves the highest responsibility, will reward the least to the greatest of labor, and will condemn all who trifle with its sacred contents.

What a fitting tribute to the Word of God. In view of these truths, with what attitude should we approach the Bible?

1. We should approach the Bible with absolute reverence for God. When we open the Bible, we are opening the mind and heart of God. Through the Scripture, God has revealed to us His thoughts, positions and perspectives about Himself, about us and about all areas of life. As we read the Scripture, we should realize that when the Bible speaks, God speaks. As such, we should harbor the greatest degree of respect and honor for God and for His Word (Psalms 19:7-14).

2. We should approach the Bible with a hunger for the knowledge of God. Just as we make food a priority for our bodies, we should make the Scripture a priority as nourishment for our souls. We should maintain a healthy appetite for the Scripture, and we should satisfy that appetite by spending time reading the Bible each and every day. The more Scripture we learn, the more

we will want to experience the promises of the Scripture in our lives. God has promised that those of us who have a healthy appetite for His Word will grow in maturity and experience the joy of His Holy Spirit living inside us (Matthew 5:6; 1 Peter 2:1-2).

3. We should approach the Bible with the expectation to be blessed by obeying its teachings. God loves us more than we love ourselves and the Scripture is filled with a multitude of promises of the ways the Lord will bless His people. God has promised to see to all of our needs being met (Philippians 4:19). God has promised to provide many of the desires of our hearts (Psalm 37:4; Matthew 7:7-11). As you seek to walk in God's will, read the Scripture expecting to see the promises of God manifested in your life.

Tools for Bible Study

1. Use a reliable Study Bible in either the King James Version (KJV), New King James Version (NKJV), New American Standard Version (NASB) or New International Version (NIV). These are recommended because all are good translations that attempt to provide the most accurate English rendering of the Hebrew and Greek manuscripts. In addition, these translations attempt to provide the English rendering without any denominational bias. Either of these versions (KJV, NKJV, NASB, NIV) in the Life

Application Study Bible will greatly help you to learn God's Word.

2. Use a Strong's Concordance with the Hebrew and Greek Dictionaries and a Vine's Dictionary of Biblical Words. The Hebrew and Greek languages were two of the most expressive and versatile available at the time of the writing of the Old and New Testaments. Our English language is not as expressive, therefore; some specific meanings that were stated in the Hebrew and in the Greek had to be generalized in the English because there was not an English equivalent. The best way to overcome this issue is to use a dictionary that provides the original meaning of Bible words. In addition, Strong's is a Concordance (an alphabetical index) that will help you find specific passages that deal with the many subjects addressed in the Bible. The Strong's and Vine's each have their own qualities and are a necessity for one striving to be a serious student of the Bible.

3. Select a quality Bible Handbook and Bible Dictionary. These volumes are helpful in providing background, cultural, historical and geographical information on the books, people, places and events recorded in the Bible. Unger, Holman, Revell and Kregel are four companies that produce quality Bible Handbooks and Bible Dictionaries.

4. Consider a set of Bible Commentaries. A Commentary will provide much of the same information as a Bible Handbook and a Bible Dictionary but its primary strength is its expla-

nation and interpretation of virtually every verse in the Bible, from Genesis to Revelation. The Beacon Bible Commentary (Beacon Hill Press) and the Expositor's Bible Commentary (Edited by Frank Gaebelein) are two of the better productions available.

Conclusion

Someone once said, "The quality of a man's product will be no better than the tools he has to work with." If we expect to do quality work in the study of the Scripture, we need to invest in quality study tools. Also, many of the recommended tools are available on CD or DVD that can be installed on a computer and some programs are compatible with handheld devices (phones and pda's).

The Nuts and Bolts of Bible Study

All Bible study activities can be categorized under one of three headings; Observation, Interpretation or Application. Let us explore each of these categories.

1. Observation
The first skill you want to develop is your ability to discern the details in and around a particular passage of Scripture. This first step is vitally important because the more equipped you are to see the details of a passage, the more likely you are to accurately interpret that passage of Scripture. Following are some specific details to look for:

a. Research the answers to the key question that surround the passages being studied. Examples questions are: Who is the author of the book containing your study passage and when was it written? What was the circumstance of the author as he wrote the book? What was the relationship between the author and the recipients? What is the primary theme or message of the book? Who were the recipients of the book? What were the cultural, political and religious circumstances the recipients were living under, at the time of the writing?

Answer these questions relating to the specific verse or verses you are studying: Are any things said immediately before the passage you are studying that influence what is said in those verses? Are there any persons, places or words in the verses you do not understand? The answers to these questions will help you see the larger picture and better understand the context in which your study verses were spoken.

b. Look for key words in a passage. They are usually found in the forms of verbs and nouns and sometimes are indicated by the repetition of a particular word or the repetition of the same ideas using synonyms. 1 Corinthians chapter 13 is an example of a repetition using the word "charity" or "love"; depending upon the version of Scripture you are using. Psalm 5, verses 1-3 use the word *pray* or one of its synonyms at least five times. Repetitions of these types help us discover the main idea being presented by the author.

c.   Be alert to advisements, warnings, commands, encouragements and promises being made. Many of these statements will be made as imperatives or direct commands.

d.   Look for purpose statements and cause/effect relationships such as found in Luke 18:1 where Jesus states the purpose for telling of the parable of the "Judge and the Widow." Pay attention to conditional statements such as John 15:7 where Jesus says, "If you abide in me…" Those grammatical relationships are important to the discovery of the primary message being conveyed through a passage of Scripture.

e.   Look for contrasts and comparisons between one thing and another. Notice the contrast between the righteous and the unrighteous in 1 Peter 3:12. In Jeremiah 20:9, he made a comparison by saying that God's Word was like fire shut up in his bones. There are numerous instances where the Bible uses natural things to illustrate spiritual truths. Be aware of the use of these literary devices.

f.   Pay attention to the use of questions. A writer may use a question to introduce an idea, to challenge the thinking of his audience, to create a teachable moment, or to summarize a point. Sometimes the question will require an answer such as in Luke 10:36 where Jesus asked, *"So which of these three do you think was neighbor to him who fell among thieves?"* At other times the writer will use a rhetorical question that does not require an answer, such as in Romans 6:1 where Paul said, *"What shall we say then? Shall we continue in sin that grace may abound?"* None of the hearers had to respond for the answer was obviously a resounding No!

Conclusion

In Bible study, as in any other effort to investigate a matter, our first task is to observe the details. We must observe the content before we can discover the intent. We must discern the details before we can determine what they mean. Be diligent at sharpening your eye to see the details in and around any portion of Scripture so that you properly discern the content of a chosen text.

2. Interpretation

The interpretative step of Bible study is tremendously important because inappropriate applications of Scripture usually begin at this stage. Remember that everything written in the Bible was put there for our awareness, but not everything in it is specifically for us to emulate. Everything in the Scripture is descriptive (describing what happened), but everything in the Bible is not prescriptive (prescribing the same behavior for us today). Following are two rules that reign supreme in the pursuit of accurate interpretation of Scripture:

a.   Always start by determining the kind of behavior a passage of Scripture required of those to whom it was first written. When Moses gave the Hebrew people the commandments found in the books of Exodus through Deuteronomy, what behaviors were expected of them? When Paul instructed the Corinthians in his two letters to them, what behaviors were expected? Always make this determination first as you seek to determine the meaning of a particular portion of Scripture. The meaning to the original audience provides the proper interpretation of the passage.

b. After accomplishing step one, proceed to determine what behavior that passage of Scripture is requiring of us today. You should never attempt to make the present-day application before discovering the meaning of the text to those to whom it was originally written.

During this interpretative stage you may need to use some of the following tools:

a. A Hebrew and Greek Dictionary to define words.

b. A Bible Dictionary or Encyclopedia to gather additional facts about a person, place, concept, ceremony or event mentioned in your study passage.

c. A Bible Commentary that provides background information on your study verses and helps with the interpretation of that passage.

As you proceed through the interpretative stage of your Bible study, pray and meditate on certain passages such as Psalm 19:7-14; Psalm 119:18; and

Psalm 139:23-24. As you open your heart to the will of God, the Holy Spirit will open your mind to the Word of God.

3. Application

The observation, interpretation and application of a passage of Scripture are tremendously important steps and each is as intertwined with the other as "Siamese Twins." They are so connected that failure in one area causes distortion in the other. All Bible study is to produce Christ-likeness in the student, and that is only accomplished when the teachings of the text are properly understood and then properly applied by the Christian. That is the primary message of two key Bible passages. 2 Timothy 2:15 states that the study of the Scripture is to enable the student to engage in a lifestyle that meets the approval of God. 2 Timothy 3:16-17 teaches that the Scripture should cause the student to become mature in his Christian faith and prepared for a good and useful life. Upon reaching the application stage of your Bible study, consider these nine questions and see how many are answered by the details of your study passage (Questions taken from *Living by the Book* by Howard and William Hendricks).

- Is there an example to follow?
- Is there a sin to avoid?
- Is there a promise to claim?
- Is there a prayer to repeat?
- Is there a command to obey?
- Is there a condition to meet?
- Is there a verse to memorize?

- Is there an error to mark?
- Is there a challenge to face?

Upon answering the question or questions that apply to the particular passage you are studying, you will then be better able to determine what behavior God expects of you.

Conclusion

The study of Scripture is one of the most important duties of the Christian. The Bible provides food for our souls. The Bible waters and refreshes our spirits. The Bible fertilizes our lives and facilitates our growth and maturity. Work hard at becoming the most capable Bible student possible and, as you study and properly interpret the Scripture, you can then pursue a life of peace and blessedness by applying God's Word to your every situation.

How much time does it take to read from Genesis to Revelation? If you would read the Bible at standard pulpit speed (slow enough to be heard and understood) the reading time would be seventy-one hours. If you would break that down into minutes and divide it into 365 days, you could read the entire Bible, cover to cover, in only 12 minutes a day. Is this really too much time to spend reading about God?

—Author Unknown

Chapter 7

What About Tithes and Offerings?

Genesis 14:18-20
> *Then Melchizedek king of Salem brought out bread and wine; he was the priest of God Most High. And he blessed him and said: "Blessed be Abram of God Most High, Possessor of heaven and earth; And blessed be God Most High, Who has delivered your enemies into your hand." And he gave him a tithe of all.*

The word tithe means *a tenth* or 10%. Though the subject of money can generate a considerable amount of controversy, it is so central to our lives that each of us need to better understand the Bible's teaching on this matter. Consider these points of truth.

1. God is the Creator of the earth and everything in it. He is the Source of everything that is good and worthy of our possession (Psalm 24:1; James 1:16-17).

2. We came into this world with nothing and when we leave we will not take any material things with us (Job. 1:21).

3. God is the only Person who can claim owner-ship to anything. We must understand that we are stewards and caretakers of the money and material items we possess. Everything in our care has been loaned to us for our usage while we are on this earth. As we live on this earth, we can become unable to drive a car, unable to use a remote control, unable to go to the store and spend money or unable to use any other earthly possession. When we decease, the material items we called "our own" will probably be given to others. Even a wife or a husband can become the spouse of another after a person passes away. The things we possess and the persons intimately connected to us, in reality, are "God's property" on loan to us (1 Chronicles 29:10-14).

4. The only thing we can attach such a word as "mine" to is sin. Everything we have that is worth having was given to us as a blessing from God. The only thing we have that was not given to us by God is sin and every day of our lives, God is attempting to wrest sin from our hearts and hands (Romans 3:23; I John 1:8-9).

5. God is the One who gives us the mental and physical abilities to enter into the marketplace

and exchange our skills and abilities for money. Some of us are employees while others are business owners and independent contractors. Some have reached retirement and now wait each month for a check to come through the mail or for the transferral of monies by direct deposit. Regardless of whether we are out earning money or at home waiting for it to be transferred to us, all of it belongs to God and we would not have the money if it were not for Him (John 15:5; Acts 17:28).

Conclusion

The giving of tithes and offerings is the only means of financial support defined in Scripture for God's Ministry, as it operates here on the earth. We need to accept the fact that our ability to earn money and every dollar gained from our efforts is a gift to us from God. When we accept this fact, we acquire a greater desire to obey the instructions in Scripture that teach us how to be good stewards of God's money.

The History of Tithes and Offerings

1. Abraham's nephew Lot and a number of other persons and their possessions were taken captive during a military conflict. After hearing of it, Abraham and his trained men engaged in a fight with their captors and regained the freedom of all the persons and possessions. As Abraham

returned from the battle, he encountered a mysterious person named Melchizedek. Consider the details of this encounter as recorded in Genesis 14:18-20:

a. Melchizedek was the King of Salem, the city that would later be called Jerusalem (City of Peace). As king, Melchizedek was the leader of all of the civil and governmental affairs of Salem.

b. Melchizedek was also the Priest of Salem and his priesthood was ordained by God. He not only led the governmental affairs, but he was also the leader of the spiritual affairs of Salem that were performed to bring honor and glory to God.

c. Melchizedek presented himself to Abraham and offered him bread and wine.

d. Melchizedek blessed Abraham and, on behalf of God, pronounced the goodness of God upon Abraham that pointed to Abraham enjoying both spiritual and material prosperity.

e. Abraham in turn gave Melchizedek a tithe of all that he had gained from his victory over the kings while liberating Lot and the others.

Though these are the events that occurred during the interaction between Melchizedek and Abraham, consider the spiritual implications of these matters:

a. Melchizedek was a minister of God and he led a ministry that was ordained by God. The ministry operated on the earth and it required earthly resources, such as money, to carry out its God-given functions and mandates.

b. Melchizedek represented far more than what met the eye. He was an Old Testament person whose life and ministry foreshadowed or predicted the person and ministry of Jesus Christ. Christ would come as the King of the Jews and that kingdom was centralized in Jerusalem (Zechariah 9:9; Matthew 21:1-11). Christ was prophesied to come as the Prince of Peace (Isaiah 9:6-7). Christ would offer bread and wine and would show how those elements represented His body and His blood that would be sacrificed for the sins of the world (Matthew 26:26-27).

c. Christ would become our High Priest after the order or pattern of Melchizedek; an eternal priesthood (Hebrews 5:1-11; 7:1-10).

d. Abraham realized that Melchizedek was God's representative and the ministry led by Melchizedek represented God's Kingdom on the earth. Therefore, Abraham gave Melchizedek tithes to support the advancement of God's Kingdom on the earth.

e. Abraham understood the concept of sowing and reaping, therefore he sowed material things into God's ministry knowing God would bless him for doing so. He also was confident God would meet his material and spiritual needs and that God would give him some of the desires of his heart.

2. On one occasion, as Jacob was travelling from Beersheba to Haran, he stopped for the night in a place called Luz. That night as he slept, God appeared to him in a dream and made various promises to him. God promised to give his people the very land he slept on and God promised to make Jacob's descendents as numerous as the grains of sand on the ground around him. God promised that Jacob's offspring would be so blessed that they would become a source of blessings to the entire earth. God further promised to protect Jacob and to supply his every need. After awaking from that dream and realizing he had been in the presence of the Lord and that he had been offered many promises from God, Jacob made a vow to God. He stated that if God would bless him in such ways as putting food on his table and clothing on his back, Jacob promised to give God a tenth or a tithe of everything he received.

These two occasions of Abraham giving tithes to Melchizedek and Jacob's vow to give God a tenth of all of his increase are the first times this practice of tithing is mentioned in the Bible. Each of these incidents occurred years before the institution of the Law of Moses and many centuries before the beginning of the Church Age. The period of Law began in Exodus 20; around 1500 B. C., and it ended on the day of Pentecost. Consider the practice of tithing during that period of time.

Tithing During the Period of the Law

1. God declared that a tenth of everything the Hebrew people gained belonged to Him (Leviticus 27:30-32; Deuteronomy 14:22-23). God wanted them to understand that, in reality, the entire earth was His possession and that He was the source of every good thing that they received in this life (Psalms 24:1). God wanted the Hebrews to be mindful that He and He alone gave them the ability to get wealth and accumulate assets (Deuteronomy 8:18).

2. Of the 12 tribes of Israel, the tribe of Levi was designated to attend to the tabernacle and provide spiritual leadership for the nation. The priests would come from this tribe. The choir members, the ushers, and all of the tabernacle workers were from the tribe of Levi. As such, the Levites were not permitted to work for any income. The tithes from the other tribes were to be used to support the daily needs of the Levites, their families and to provide for the financial needs of the tabernacle. (Leviticus 1:47-54; Nehemiah 10:35-38). During the days of Solomon, the tabernacle was replaced with the temple. Its construction was massive, it required a far larger staff than the tabernacle and its financial needs were multiple times more.

3. Since the tithe belonged to God, the refusal of an Israelite to give his tithes was tantamount to "robbing God" (Malachi 3:8-9). When this happened, the priests and the Levites abandoned the temple to find means to feed their families.

Consequently, the nation drifted into idolatry, immorality and other sins due to the absence of strong spiritual leadership. God rebuked the Hebrew people for their failure to give their tithes and offerings to fund the financial needs of the temple and to support the priests and Levites. Along with the rebuke, God promised blessings to those who would be faithful in giving their tithes and offerings to support His kingdom on the earth (Malachi 3:10-12). Consider the promised blessings for those who would be faithful and obedient:

a. God promised to open the "windows of heaven" for them. This phrase indicated that God would continually supply their every need and many of the desires of their hearts and that He would do it in abundance (verse 10).
b. God promised that He would protect their crops from insects, drought and all other threats so that they would always have a bountiful supply of food (verse 11).
c. God promised to bless the Hebrews in such a way that they would be admired and looked up to by other nations (verse 12).

Tithing as Addressed by Jesus

The only mentioning of giving of tithes by Jesus was a reference in Matthew 23:23 and Luke 14:42 and the setting was the same in both passages. The Scribes and Pharisees were the most religious of all the groups that adhered to the belief system of the Jewish people. These groups were very meticulous in their observance of the feasts, ceremonies and rituals of their religion. They gave a tithe of everything they accumulated right down to the herbs and spices they planted in gardens around their homes. On the other hand, they neglected the foundational command-ments of loving God with their entire hearts and loving their neighbors as themselves. Jesus rebuked the Scribes and Pharisees for their failures, but He commended them wherever He could and giving of tithes was one area Jesus could say to them, "well done."

Tithing as Addressed in the Book of Acts

Christianity grew out of Judaism; the religion of the Jewish people. Jesus was Jewish and so were the men He called as His Apostles. As Christ and His Apostles gained a following, most were Jewish. On the Day of Pentecost, about 5000 persons believed the gospel and became Christians. Each of those persons either had been born into the Jewish family or had converted to the religion of the Jews. All throughout the book of Acts, there are numerous records of Jewish persons and proselytes becoming Christians and many of those Jews were from the Judaic lead-ership (Acts 6:7). As those persons converted and became Christian, they were already accustomed to giving their tithes and offerings in support of either the temple in Jerusalem or their local synagogues. Those persons understood the Church to be the New

Movement of God on the earth. As such, the Church would have the same financial needs as the Temple and the synagogues. The Church had ministers who needed to give themselves to fulltime service. The Church practiced love by meeting the daily physical needs of its less-fortunate members. The Jews who rejected Christianity controlled the Temple and the Synagogues, magnifying the need of the Church to have adequate facilities to hold worship services and teaching sessions. There was no need to give specific instructions about bringing tithes and offerings into the storehouse. The Jewish Christian understood that the Church was now the Storehouse to which he was to bring his tithe.

Passages Related to Giving in the New Testament

1 Corinthians 9:1-15

In these fifteen verses, Paul instructed the Corinthian Church in its responsibility to provide a sufficient salary for their pastor to allow him to give fulltime service to the ministry. In verse 9, Paul quoted from the Law, as recorded in Deuteronomy 25:4, to strengthen his teaching to the Corinthians. In verse 14, he emphatically stated that, *"The Lord has commanded that those who preach the gospel should live from the gospel."* This scenario was an exact parallel to the Priests and Levites of the Old Covenant receiving their living from the tithes and offerings of the Hebrews so they could fully commit themselves to the care of the people and to the maintenance of the Tabernacle and later the Temple.

1 Corinthians 16:1-4

In this text, Paul instructed the Church at Corinth concerning raising offerings to help the Church in Jerusalem that was financially challenged (Romans 15:26). The largest concentration of Christians was in Jerusalem, the same place where the largest concentration of persecutors of Christians resided. The anti-Christian Jews of Jerusalem exercised great influence over the business and economics of the region. As long as they paid the taxes demanded by Caesar, Rome stayed out of their personal and religious matters. In addition, Orthodox Jew believed the persecution of Christianity was his religious duty. Consequently, the Church at Jerusalem suffered financially. The first duty of the Corinthian Christian was to take care of the financial needs of his and her church-home, and that was accomplished by the tithe. The offering Paul called for was for contributions over and above the tithes. The tithe is 10% of each dollar earned. The offering is any amount above the tithe anyone is able to give, according to how one has prospered. These instructions do not nullify the practice of tithing carried over from the Old Testament but they compliment them.

2 Corinthians 9:6-9

This passage is a favorite of those who attempt to relegate the practice of tithing to Old Testament times. The giving of offerings in this passage was a request for additional giving beyond the tithes that would go to needy congregations in Macedonia and in Jerusalem. This is easily seen by doing a careful study of 2 Corinthians 8:1-9:15. Doing so places 2 Corinthians 9:6-8 in its proper context, and that context is, of the Corinthian Church members giving special offerings to help a distant congregation after they had given their tithes to care for their own church home.

<u>1 Timothy 5:17-18</u>

In this passage, the apostle Paul instructed Timothy in the establishment of the financial protocols of the Church at Ephesus as it related to salary for pastors. This Church had a group of Elders who gave leadership to the church, of which some were teacher/preachers and others were not. Paul instructed that all elders were to be compensated but those who ministered the Word of God were to receive significantly more than those who did not. Again, as he did to the Church at Corinth (1 Corinthians 9:9), Paul quoted Deuteronomy 25:4 to charge the Church at Ephesus in its financial obligations toward those who provide their ministerial leadership. In addition, Paul quoted the words of Jesus in Luke 10:7 concerning the Minister being deserving of his salary. This scenario is a direct parallel with Old Testament practice of the priests and Levites being cared for by the tithes and offerings of the eleven tribes.

Conclusion

For at least 1500 years, the Nation of Israel served as God's primary instrument on this earth, through which He extended His grace to all humankind. Toward the end of that period, God manifested Himself in human form in the person of Jesus Christ. During His ministry, Jesus promised to establish another ministry that would replace Israel as God's primary representative in the earth, and that ministry is the Church (Matthew 16:18). Just as Israel was a ministry that had a Temple, a staff of leaders and religious workers and their associated expenses, so does the Church. God, in His wisdom, established the practice of His people giving tithes and offerings of their resources to provide for the needs of the religious workers and for the Temple in which they served. Would God do any less for the Church? Certainly not! Every Jewish income earner who became a member of the Body of Christ was expected to support the Church with his resources, just as he had done under the Law. When carefully examined in context, it will be discovered that none of the instructions to the Churches about giving money nullify the practice of tithing that was to be carried over from the Old Testament.

When we place our contribution in the collection plate, we are not giving to the Lord; we are just taking our hands off what belongs to Him.
—The Speaker's Quote Book

Chapter 8

What About My Church Home?

Hebrews 10:24-25
And let us consider one another in order to stir up love and good works, not forsaking the assembling of ourselves together, as is the manner of some, but exhorting one another, and so much the more as you see the Day approaching.

One of the most important decisions Christians make is their choice of the church they are going to attend. There are two primary reasons this decision is so important. First, all believers need to be able to join their energies and abilities with other Christians in order to advance God's will on the earth. Second, all believers need to be under pastoral leadership so that they can be further matured and developed in the faith. These two matters can be summarized in these two questions: What should your church expect of you? What should you expect of your church?

What Should Your Church Expect of You?

1. Spend quality time with the Lord praying for your pastor, your church leadership and your church membership. God does wonderful and miraculous things in the lives of praying saints and in the midst of churches that make prayers to God a priority.
2. Spend time at home studying the passages of Scripture your pastor preaches from during the worship services, ask the Lord to give you further understanding of the Word and ask Him to further transform your life through the sermons.
3. Be faithful in attending the teaching and preaching sessions of your church. Arrive on time, appropriately dressed and ready to make meaningful contributions toward the effectiveness of all that is going on.
4. Be faithful in the giving of your time, talents, tithes and offerings to God's church.
5. Beyond the Bible study class and worship service, pray and ask God to show you where you are to serve in the ministry. Some churches offer a class that helps members better understand their spiritual gifts and then directs them to an area of service that is best suited to those gifts and abilities.
6. Speak well of your pastor, church leaders and church members. Refrain from participating in

any conversations or activities that may contribute to a division in your church or to the damaging of another's reputation.

7.   If you become offended or hurt by someone, try to resolve your issues with that person without making the matter known to others.

What Should You Expect of Your Church?

1.   You should expect to enter into an environment where the love of God is expressed by the people and is shared in such a way that it is felt and experienced by all. There will always be individuals you may have concerns with, but it should be obvious that the pastor and leaders love God, they love one another and are influencing the congregation to do the same.

2.   You should expect to enter into an environment where there is absolute genuineness and sincerity regarding the Christian life and all that is related to it. There is always room for laughter and fun, but humor should never compromise the seriousness and the integrity of a church setting.

3.   You should expect to enter into an environment where God is honored and worshipped for who He is and for all that He does for us. The worship style of some churches is livelier and louder than others. Rituals and ceremonies may be different but your first concern is to determine the quality of the worship gatherings and look to see church leaders who lead the congregation in worship

that is genuine, sincere and where the presence of the Holy Spirit is felt.

4. You should expect to sit under the leadership of a pastor who obviously loves his wife and his family and that they are his highest priority, as he seeks to be a good pastor to them at home.

5. You should expect your pastor to have genuine love for people, especially those under his leadership. The church family should be cared for in ways that meet the needs the church is responsible for supplying. The pastor may not be personally involved in providing every aspect of pastoral care to the church members, but there should be persons who respond to the hurting, the bereaved, the sick and other individuals who are facing the various challenges of life.

6. You should expect your pastor to love the Word of God and to teach and preach the Word of God in such a way that you can understand it and apply it to your life. It should be obvious that his sermons and presentations of himself are not performances or attempts to impress anyone. His love for God's Word and his recognition of the seriousness of the responsibility of teaching and preaching the Bible should be clear to all.

7. You should expect a pastor and a church that provides you with the settings, classes, and opportunities where you can learn and grow in the Scriptures. You should also expect ministry opportunities through which you can serve and utilize your gifts and abilities.

Conclusion

One of the most important associations Christians have is their pastoral and church member relationships. Do all you can, say all you can, and pray all you can in ways that will encourage your pastor, your church leaders and your fellow church members. Give your time, your abilities and your resources in ways that contribute to the good of the church you attend. Finally, think about the following quote from an unknown author, "If everybody in my church was just like me, what kind of church would my church be?"

When the roots of trees touch, there is a substance present that reduces competition. In fact, this unknown fungus helps link roots of different tree—even of dissimilar species. A whole forest may be linked together. If one tree has access to water, another to nutrients, and a third to sunlight, the trees have the means to share with one another. Like trees in a forest, Christians in the church need and support one another.

—Reader's Digest

Chapter 9

What About The Holy Spirit?

1 John 4:12-13

> *No one has seen God at any time. If we love one another, God abides in us, and His love has been perfected in us. By this we know that we abide in Him, and He in us, because He has given us of His Spirit.*

We are living in the Age of the Holy Spirit. During the days of the Old Testament, God the Father was the prominent expression of the Trinity. During the days described by the four gospels, the Lord Jesus Christ was the prominent expression of the Trinity. Ten days before the Day of Pentecost, Jesus ascended to heaven and positioned Himself at the right hand of God the Father (Acts 1:1-9; 1 Peter 3:22). On the Day of Pentecost, the Holy Spirit descended upon the apostles and upon 108 others. Since that day, the Holy Spirit has been the prominent representative of the Trinity in the earth. Some also refer to this "Age of the Holy Spirit" as the "Dispensation of Grace" or as the "Church Age." In view of these truths, Christians should seek to gain a clear understanding of the person and the works of the Holy Spirit.

The Personality of the Holy Spirit

Psychologists say that in order for a living creature to be classified as a person, he must possess three faculties: a mind, emotions and a will. The mind points to the capacity for intelligence and decision making abilities. Emotions have to do with the ability to consciously experience feelings such as love, hate, anger and others. Possessing a will has to do with the ability to combine the activity of the mind and the influence of the emotions and to make conscious and deliberate decisions. The Holy Spirit possesses all of these faculties, and is therefore, the epitome of personality.

The Mind of the Holy Spirit

The Holy Spirit has a mind (Romans 8:27) and He knows and investigates matters that relate to God and Christ. He does so for the purpose of teaching us and opening our understanding to spiritual matters (1 Corinthians 2:11-13). He can be lied to just as the Father and Son (Acts 5:1-3). The Holy Spirit speaks to believers (Revelation 2:7), He calls persons into the ministry (Acts 13:2), He directs their ministerial activities (Acts 16:6-7) and He presides over the Church (Acts 20:28).

The Emotions of the Holy Spirit

Just as a parent can become grieved when a son or daughter is going astray, the Holy Spirit has the same emotional capacity in relation to our obedience and disobedience (Ephesians 4:30; Acts 10:19-21). The Holy Spirit can be resisted (Acts 7:51), blasphemed (Matthew 12:31) and insulted (Hebrews 10:29).

The Will of the Holy Spirit

The Holy Spirit has a will and He uses it to influence and order the activities of believers (Acts 16:6-11). He uses His will to determine which spiritual gifts are given to believers (1 Corinthians 12:11). He exercises His will by guiding the lives of believers (John 16:13), by performing miracles (Acts 8:39) and by interceding to the Father on our behalf (Romans 8:26).

The Equality of the Holy Spirit

The Holy Spirit is equal to the Holy Father and the Holy Son in essence, character, in substance, and in all other aspects that make each divine, eternal and deserving of our worship. Consider these examples of ways in which the equality of the Holy Spirit is demonstrated.

The Holy Spirit was equally involved in the creation of the world, along with the Father (Genesis 1:2). He moved upon men and inspired them to write the Scriptures (2 Peter 1:20-21). He caused the birth of Jesus by a Virgin (Luke 1:34). The Holy Spirit is called the Spirit of Yahweh (Heb. 10:15-17) and is given equal status with the Father and the Son in the baptism formula (Matthew 28:19) and in Paul's benediction (2 Corinthians 13:14).

The Saving Work of the Holy Spirit

Not only was the Holy Spirit centrally involved in the creation of the world and in the birth of the Savior, He is also the Agent of the new birth of the believer (Titus 3:5). God the Father planned our salvation before the world began (Ephesians 1:3-4). The Lord Jesus Christ came into this world and paid the redemption price for salvation by shedding His blood for the sins of the world (John 1:29; 1 John 2:1-2). God the Father is on His throne in heaven and the resurrected Christ is stationed at His right hand of power (Acts 7:55). The Holy Spirit is the representative of the Trinity who is at work in this earth implementing the plans of the Father that were provided by the Son. How does the Holy Spirit exercise His role in the eternal plan of God?

Regeneration

When an individual repents of his sins, places his faith in the good news concerning Jesus Christ and asks the Lord to save him, the Holy Spirit saves him, regenerates him, and gives him eternal life (Titus 3:3-5; 1 Corinthians 6:9-11).

Indwelling

The Holy Spirit comes to live in the heart and soul of the new believer. He conjoins His Holy Spirit with the believer's human spirit and transforms the individual into a child of God. All Christians have the Holy Spirit living inside of them, and this indwelling happens immediately at conversion. There is no such thing as a person being a Christian, but lacking the indwelling presence of the Holy Spirit (Romans 8:9; 1 Corinthians 3:16; 1 John 4:12-13). Again, this indwelling places the Holy Spirit within the believer, it gives him his Christian identity and it happens once for all time.

Baptism

The word *baptize* means to overwhelm something by placing it completely inside of something else. The baptism of the Holy Spirit takes the believer out of the kingdom of darkness and places that person into the body of Christ. The new believer becomes overwhelmed with Christ by being immersed in Him (1 Corinthians 12:13; Romans 6:3-4; Colossians 2:11-12). Again, the indwelling places the Holy Spirit in the heart of the believer while the baptism of the Holy Spirit places the believer into the body of Christ and each occurs once for all time.

Filling

The filling of the Holy Spirit can be described as the influence and control of the Spirit in the life of the Christian to the point that the believer's thoughts, words and deeds are perfectly in harmony with the teachings of Scripture. To say it another way, when we are filled with the Holy Spirit, we manifest holiness in all we think, say and do. Let me reiterate, the indwelling and the baptism of the Holy Spirit happens at conversion once for all time. On the other hand, the filling of the Holy Spirit happens when a person receives Christ, but in order to remain filled, it must be sought moment by moment and day by day. This is what the Apostle Paul refers to in Ephesians 5:18. The statement in that verse, "be filled" is a direct command to Christians who have already experienced the indwelling and baptism of the Holy Spirit. Those persons were already converts to Christ but they were commanded to seek to live every moment of life under the influence of the Holy Spirit. Doing so would enable their lives to consistently manifest the fruit of the Holy Spirit. This fruit is described in Galatians 5:22-23, and its predominance in a person's life is the only reliable way to determine if a person has the Holy Spirit living in his heart.

In addition, the filling of the Holy Spirit also has to do with God empowering believers to perform special services or activities. In Acts 9:17, Paul was saved and filled with the Holy Spirit at his conversion. In Acts 13:8-11, he was filled or empowered by the Holy Spirit for the special purpose of rebuking a sorcerer named Elymas and causing him to become blind. Peter and the other apostles were converted to Christ years before, but on the Day of Pentecost the Holy Spirit filled them and empowered them to speak in the languages of the many foreigners gathered in Jerusalem that day. This was not something they did as a permanent practice but only for that occasion and the great need of the foreign Jews and proselytes to hear the Scripture in their native tongue.

Sealing

The sealing of the Holy Spirit is another one of His works that are enjoyed by all believers. By it, we are granted two primary benefits. The first is being bestowed with God's signature or mark of identification. Though it is not a visible mark, Satan and the demons are able to see and understand that each believer is God's Property (2 Corinthians 1:21-22; Ephesians 1:13).

The second expression of the sealing of the Holy Spirit is to provide security for our relationship with the Lord so that we never revert to our former condition nor lose our salvation. Not only does the Holy Spirit place us in God's family, but He also protects us from all threats to our relationship with our heavenly Father (Ephesians 4:30; Colossians 3:3; 1 John 4:4; John 10:27-30).

Additional Attributes

As was stated at the beginning of this chapter, the Holy Spirit is the representative of the Trinity at work in the earth today. He represents the Father and the Son. Therefore, He has to be of the same essence and substance as they. He has to be equal to them in every aspect so that He can do the same as they would do if they were here. After telling the apostles several times that He (Jesus) would be leaving them, they became uncomfortable. Jesus then told His disciples that He would send someone in His place who would provide them with the same sense of peace and comfort He provided; and that person was the Holy Spirit (John 14:26; 15:26; 16:7).

In addition to being the Comforter, the Holy Spirit also teaches (John 14:25-26), He testifies (John 15:26), He convicts and guides (John 16:7-15). The Holy Spirit gives commands (Acts 13:1-2), He intercedes on our behalf as we pray (Romans 8:26), and He does a host of other things on behalf of every child of God.

Conclusion

Some people believe they have good reason to question the personality and preeminence of the Holy Spirit. When the descriptions of Him given in the Bible are examined, most people relinquish their unbelief and accept the Holy Spirit for the divine Person He is. From the passages identified in this chapter that focus on the mind, emotional capacity, and the exercising of will of the Holy Spirit, we should readily see that not only is He the third person of the Trinity, but that He is equal to the Father, and to the Son. As such, the Holy Spirit is the personification and essence of personality. Without Him, we would not be the creatures we are, possessing all of the faculties that give us personhood and personality.

It is said that a certain guide lived in the deserts of Arabia who never lost his way. He carried with him a homing pigeon with a vey fine cord attached to one of its legs. When in doubt as to which path to take, he threw the bird into the air. The pigeon quickly strained at the cord to fly in the direction of home, and thus led the guide accurately to his goal. Because of this unique practice he was known as the "dove man." So, too, the Holy Spirit, the heavenly Dove, is willing and able to direct us in the narrow way that leads to the more abundant life if in humble self-denial we submit to His unerring supervision.

—The Speaker's Quote Book

Chapter <u>10</u>

What About Sharing My Faith with Others?

John 4:28, 29, 39

> *The woman then left her waterpot, went her*
> *way into the city, and said to the men, "Come,*
> *see a Man who told me all things that I ever*
> *did. Could this be the Christ?" And many of*
> *the Samaritans of that city believed in Him*
> *because of the word of the woman who testi-*
> *fied, "He told me all that I ever did."*

Someone once said that Christians were "beggars who had found bread, telling other beggars, where they can find bread." This proverbial statement captures the essence of the responsibility of believers to reach out to unbelievers and to tell them about the goodness and love of God. Babies may be born to Christian parents, but no one is born already a Christian. A Christian is a person who has made a conscious and voluntary decision to repent of his sins and place his faith in the good news about Jesus Christ. That good news is that God demonstrated His love for this world by giving the greatest gift possible, the gift of His Son. The gospel proclaims that Jesus was born of a Virgin, lived a sinless life, performed many miracles, died on a cross for the sins of the world, was buried, arose from the dead three days later, ascended to heaven and one day is coming back again. When an individual repents and believes this gospel message, that person is brought into a right relationship with God and becomes a Christian (Rom. 10:9). This relationship is the greatest that a human can experience. Therefore, the greatest act of love a Christian can show another person is to pray for that person and then actively seek that person's conversion to Christ.

Two Key New Testament Passages that Command Evangelism and Discipleship

Matthew 28:18-20 and Acts 1:8

Jesus had just spent three-and-a-half years teaching His apostles and preparing them for the ministry that each would be responsible to carry out. He then expressed His love for humankind in the greatest possible way by giving His life as a sacrifice for the sins of the world. For three days and three nights, Jesus' credibility hung in the balances as many thought that His death would be the end of His existence. Jesus then performed what may be the greatest miracle of all time when He raised Himself from the dead (John 10:14-18). The words of Matthew 28:18-20 were the first recorded statements made by the Lord immediately after His resurrection. One would assume that whatever He would say to His disciples first would be words of supreme importance. Not only were those words exceedingly important but they summarized the twofold purpose for the establishment of the Church on the earth and those two reasons are *Evangelism* and *Discipleship*. As such, these two mandates are also the two primary matters all Christians should be involved.

Evangelism

Lifestyle Evangelism

Wherever we are going within the confines of our daily routine, we should be reaching out to others with the message of God's love for them. There are many places we regularly go such as, for a walk in the neighborhood, to work, to the mall, to the barber shop. As we go throughout our daily routine, we encounter numerous individuals who need to know the Lord as their Savior. We are to seize those opportunities to be of godly influence on both strangers and on persons we know and have rapport. We are to leverage those personal relationships for the cause of Christ (John 1:35-42).

Intentional Evangelism

We are to reach out to unsaved persons with the intent of telling them about God's saving grace. We need to remind ourselves of how good God is to us. We need to realize that God wants to save and bless others just as He has saved and blessed us. One of the most important ways we express our love for God is by telling others how they can have a personal relationship with Jesus Christ. We can follow-up with persons who are willing to provide us with their contact information. We should reach out to unsaved family members and friends of persons connected to our church families. Churches can stage activities and schedule ministry events that will attract unsaved persons. We can actively participate in local, regional and global evangelism efforts and we can contribute money to help spread the Gospel.

Discipleship

After individuals enter into the Christian family, we are to help them grow and mature to the point where they can then begin influencing others to give their lives to the Lord. Discipleship comes from the word "discipline", and we are to teach new believers the doctrines of the Bible so that each engages in a lifestyle that is disciplined (ordered and regulated) by the example of Jesus Christ and by the Holy Scriptures. Following is a list of ways in which we are to disciple new believers in the Christian faith:

1. We are to see that new believers are given the truth of Scripture so that they are liberated from all forms of bondage (John 8:31-32).
2. We are to help new converts develop a new perspective on life that comes from an entirely new way of thinking (Romans 12:2). This new

way of thinking is sometimes called the development of a "Biblical World View" (looking at the things in the world as God does).

3. We are to help new believers better understand the importance of ridding their lives of all activities that are contrary to God's will (Hebrews 12:1-2).

4. We are to make sure new Christians are being edified, equipped and empowered for Christian service in the areas of their gifts and abilities (Ephesians 4:11-12).

What are some of the things you need to do to begin sharing your faith with others?

1. Sit down and write out a description of the person you were before you were saved, what happened when you gave your life to the Lord and what God has done in your life since you have been saved.

2. Summarize the main details into a three to five minute presentation.

3. Identify relatives, friends, co-workers and others you may come in contact with who need to receive Christ as Savior.

4. Begin praying for those persons to be receptive to your testimony.

5. Pray to God for His wisdom and then reach out to others and let God use your testimony to make an impact upon their lives.

6. Always remember that you are not responsible for the desired results from people you share

the gospel. You are only responsible for sharing the good news about Jesus with them. God will produce the results in the lives of those whose hearts open to Him (1 Corinthians 3:6-7; Romans 10:9-10).

Conclusion

Following is a paraphrase of the combined messages of Matthew 28:18-20 and Acts 1:8:

Jesus said "In view of the fact that I have all power and authority both in heaven and in earth, and you have that same Holy Spirit power living in your hearts, as you go through your daily routine, tell others about My love for them. Help them to become saved by My grace, and help them to grow and become mature Christians. See to each experiencing the blessings of water baptism and remember that, you have the provision and the protection of the Father, the Son and the Holy Spirit with you, wherever you go."

This is the essence of our responsibilities of sharing our faith in God with others. As we do, God will bless our efforts and use us to help others come to know Him and then help them to grow up in Him.

At age 12, Robert Louis Stevenson was looking out into the dark from his upstairs window watching a man lighting the streetlamps. Stevenson's governess came into the room and asked what he was doing. He replied, "I am watching a man cut

holes in the darkness." I see this as a marvelous picture of what our task should be as sharers of God's light—people who are busy cutting holes in the spiritual darkness of our world.

—Illustrations Unlimited

Conclusion

There is no greater life experience any person can have than to enjoy his days on this earth with a personal and intimate relationship with the Lord. Many persons receive Jesus as their Savior but fail to gain the maximum benefit from that relationship. Sometimes this occurs because they do not receive the attention and instruction that can help them become mature in the Lord. This book was written with this matter as its major concern. I trust that your reading of "What Now Lord?" has answered some of your questions and has given you the direction that will help you live the abundant life.

Now to Him who is able to do exceedingly abundantly above all that we ask or think, accordingly to the power that works in us. To Him be glory in the church by Christ Jesus to all generations, forever and ever, Amen.
—The Apostle Paul in Ephesians 3:20-21

For Further Reading

Jensen's Survey of the Old Testament and Jensen's Survey of the New Testament by Irving L Jensen (Moody Press). *Two volumes that give a through analysis of each book of the Bible.*

Lessons From a Life Coach by Crawford W. Loritts, Jr. (Moody Press). *A daily devotional that keeps the believer focused on Christ and stimulates growth and maturity.*

Living by the Book by Howard and William Hendricks (Moody Press). *A manual, for more mature believers, on studying and understanding the Bible.*

Moody Handbook of Theology by Paul Enns (Moody Press). *Provides in-depth information on the major doctrines of the Christian Church and on a host of other biblical and theological matters.*

The Complete Works of E. M. Bounds on Prayer by E. M. Bounds (Baker Books). *A classic on developing a more intimate relationship with the Lord through prayer.*

The New Evidence that Demands a Verdict by Josh McDowell (Thomas Nelson Publishers). *Answers the questions of those skeptical and critical of the Bible and Christianity.*

The New Joy of Discovery by Oletta Ward (Augsburg Fortress). *A manual, for new believers, on studying and understanding the Bible.*

Vine's Expository Dictionary of Biblical Words by W. E. Vine (Thomas Nelson Publishers). *A resource that provides the Hebrew and Greek meanings of key Bible words.*

You Can Trust the Bible by Erwin Lutzer (Moody Press). *Seven evidences that substantiate the accuracy and authority of the Bible.*

Your Thoughts and Feedback

D r. Woods would enjoy hearing your thoughts, suggestions and concerns regarding this book. He would love to hear what this writing has meant to you. You may respond through the following means:

Ministry with Excellence
Dr. Michael D. Woods
P. O. Box 870523
Stone Mountain, GA 30087

www.mwenow.com

DrWoods@mwenow.com

Contact the Author

If you are interested in scheduling Dr. Woods for a speaking engagement, as a preacher during a Worship Service or to facilitate a Seminar or Workshop, he can be reached at 770-413-3700, at DrWoods@mwenow.com or through his ministry website www.mwenow.com. Dr. Woods and his staff at Ministry with Excellence seek to Encourage Senior Pastors, Equip Associate Ministers, Empower Church Leaders and Edify Church Members to help each serve with excellence in his and her respective roles. The results are individual efficiency and effectiveness that contributes to sustained spiritual, numerical and financial growth in the churches wherein these persons lead and serve.

Printed in the United States
134506LV00001B/262-411/P